Contents

Revised Edition

Copyright © 1957, 1993, 2007 by Alfred Publishing Co., Inc.
All rights reserved. Printed in USA.

Cover guitar photo courtesy of Taylor Guitars.

Alfred Publishing Co., Inc.
16320 Roscoe Blvd., Suite 100
P.O. Box 10003
Van Nuys, CA 91410-0003
alfred.com

Book
ISBN-10: 0-7390-4892-9   ISBN-13: 978-0-7390-4892-4

Book and CD
ISBN-10: 0-7390-4891-0   ISBN-13: 978-0-7390-4891-7

CD
ISBN-10: 0-7390-4941-0   ISBN-13: 978-0-7390-4941-9

What You Should Know Before Starting This Book

If you have completed Books 1 and 2 of *Alfred's Basic Guitar Method* (or other equivalent books), you will know the following about playing single notes on the guitar. Make sure you can play these exercises perfectly before continuing.

Key of C, basic note values:

Key of G, basic note values and rests (remember that all F's are played as F♯'s):

Key of F, eighth notes and eighth rests (remember: all B's are played as B♭'s):

Key of A minor, dotted quarter notes:

Fragment from *Hungarian Dance*:

Franz Liszt

Key of E minor, dotted eighths and sixteenths (all F's are played as F♯'s):

Triplets:

High notes in the key of D (F's and C's are played as F♯'s and C♯'s):

Syncopation:

4

Before continuing further, make sure you know the following chords, their primary bass notes (roots) and alternate bass notes. You should also be able to recognize the chords when they are written out in notes.

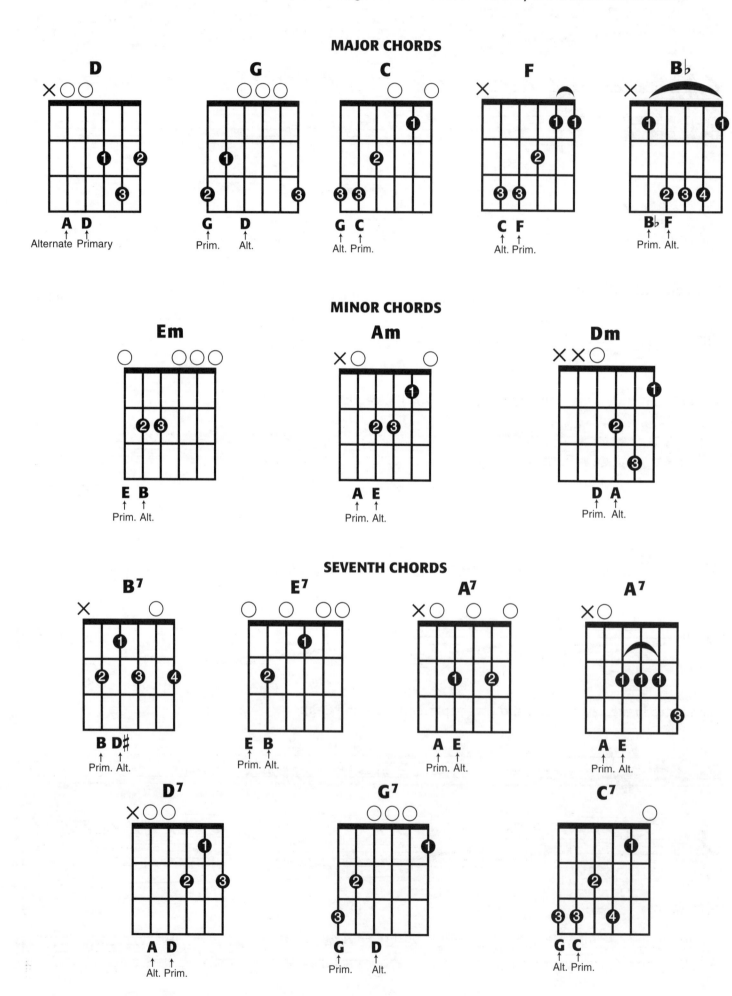

Chord Exercises

Make sure you can play the following chord exercises without missing a beat:

Key of C Major

Key of A Minor

Key of F Major

Key of E Minor

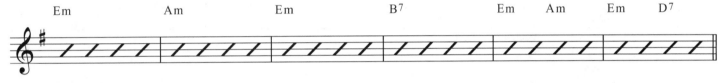

Key of G Major

Key of D Major

Key of C Major

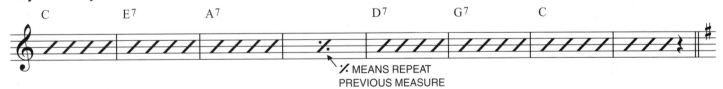

✗ MEANS REPEAT
PREVIOUS MEASURE

Key of G Major

The above exercises can be played in various ways:

1. Strumming once for each slash / .

2. Substituting a primary bass note for the first beat of each measure.

3. Substituting a primary bass note for the first beat of each measure and an alternate bass note for the third beat of each measure.

Sixteenth Notes

Sixteenth notes are black notes with two flags added to the stems: ♪ or

Generally, when two or more sixteenth notes are played, they are joined with two beams:

Sixteenth notes are played four to a beat, twice as fast as eighth notes and four times as fast as quarter notes. Use alternate picking when playing sixteenth notes.

4 quarter notes = 8 eighth notes = 16 sixteenth notes

COUNT: 1   2   3   4   1 & 2 & 3 & 4 &   1 e & uh 2 e & uh 3 e & uh 4 e & uh

In $\frac{2}{4}$ time

1   2   1 & 2 &   1   2   1 e & uh 2 e & uh   1   2

In $\frac{3}{4}$ time

1 & 2 & 3 &   1   2   3   1 e & uh 2 e & uh 3 e & uh   1   2   3

Mixin' It Up  Track 2

Fine

D.C. al Fine

The Happy Sailor  Track 3

The pattern of an eighth note followed by two sixteenth notes is very common.
The following song illustrates this rhythm. Watch the picking carefully.

Variations on a Square Dance Tune Track 4

The rhythm of two sixteenth notes followed by an eighth note is also fairly common.
Again, watch your picking carefully.

Etude in D Track 5

Arpeggios

The notes of a chord  played in succession is an *arpeggio*.

East Side, West Side Track 6

The Man on the Flying Trapeze Track 7

Scarborough Fair (duet) Track 8

This beautiful English folk song was a big hit for Simon and Garfunkel in the 1960s. It is arranged here as a duet, and the student should learn both parts. Keep the arpeggios flowing smoothly in the second part, with fingers held down as long as possible.

The Doo-Wop Ballad

Track 9

In the 1950s a style of rock and roll ballad called *doo-wop* became very popular. This type of song featured many long held notes sung over an accompaniment of triplets, played either as chords or arpeggios. Here are a few samples of each.

Key of C

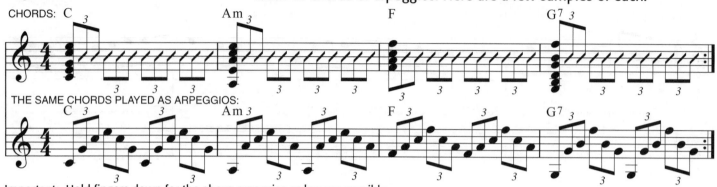

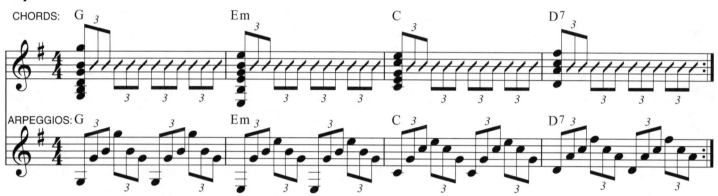

Important: Hold fingers down for the above arpeggios as long as possible.

Key of G

Key of C Chords, with Bass Notes

Key of C, with Variations

Key of G Chords, with Bass Notes

Key of G, with Variations

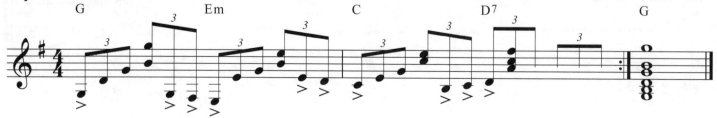

My Angel Baby (duet)

Track 10

Here is a song written in 1950s doo-wop style. Learn the melody and arpeggio-style accompaniment.

Key of A Major

The key signature of three sharps indicates the key of A major. All F's are played as F♯'s, all C's are played as C♯'s, and all G's are played as G♯'s, unless otherwise indicated by a natural sign.

When learning the two-octave A major scale below, follow the fingering carefully. Like all scales, this one should be practiced daily.

A MAJOR SCALE Track 11

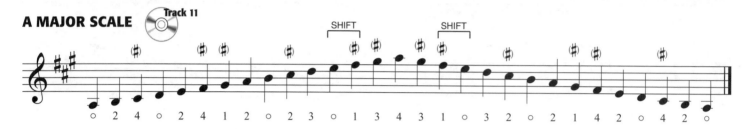

The Three Principal Chords in A with Bass Notes

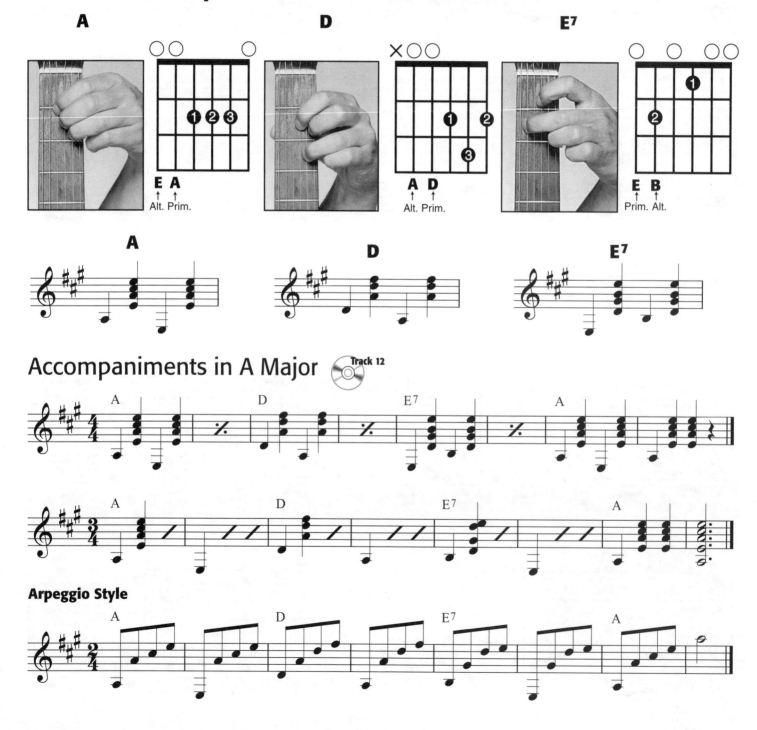

Accompaniments in A Major Track 12

Arpeggio Style

Tunes That Teach Technic No. 1

Scale Etude in A Major — Track 13

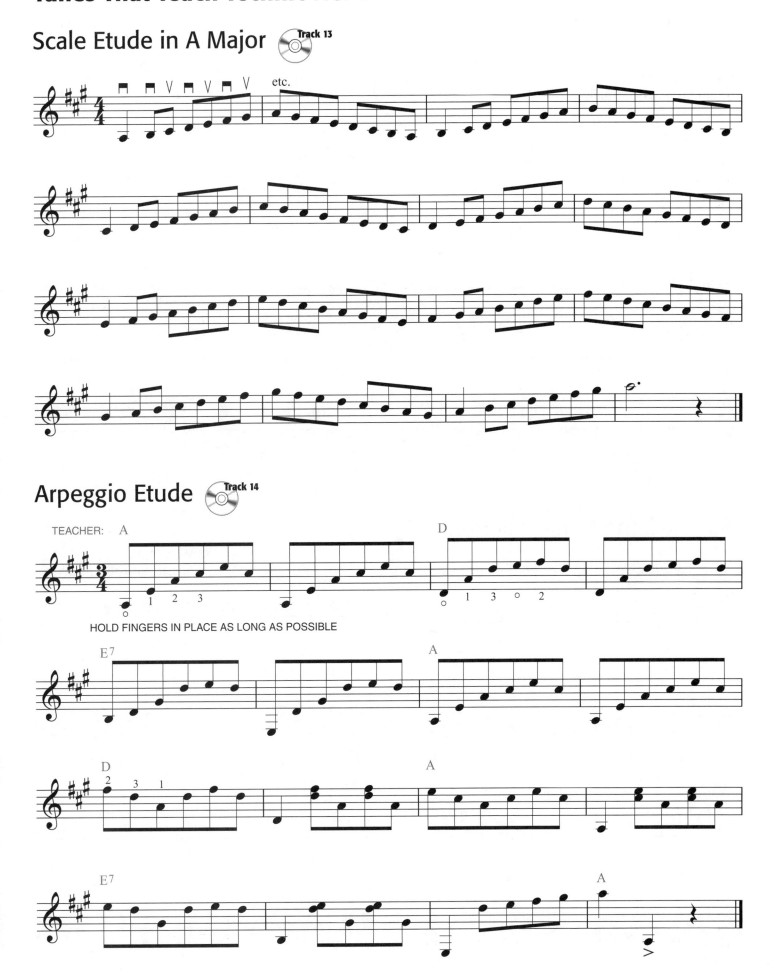

Arpeggio Etude — Track 14

HOLD FINGERS IN PLACE AS LONG AS POSSIBLE

Hard, Ain't It Hard

Track 15

Bright country tempo

Traditional

It's hard, and it's hard, ain't it hard to

love one that nev - er did love you. And it's

hard, ain't it hard, yes, it's hard, dear Lord, to

love one who nev - er could be true.

Hail, Hail, the Gang's All Here

Track 16

Words: Anon.
Music: Sir Arthur Sullivan

Like a march, in 2 (♩. = 1 beat)

Hail, hail, the gang's all here;

What the heck do we care? What the heck do we care?

Hail, hail, the gang's all here;

What the heck do we care now?

Sixteenth Note Studies in A Major

Track 17

Hammer-ons  Track 18

The *hammer-on* effect is very common, especially in rock, heavy metal, country, blues, and jazz. Every guitarist should be able to play this technique. Hammer-on means playing a note by bringing a left-hand finger down hard enough to sound the note.

A hammer-on to a *fingered* string is done like this:

1. Start with a fingered note, such as E on the 4th string, 2nd fret.

2. Strike the string with the pick while keeping the 1st finger firmly in place.

3. Then, hammer the 2nd finger down hard and fast. The F will sound.

In music notation, this is written like this:

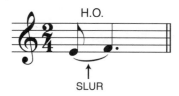

The curved line between the E and the F is called a *slur* and means that the F is not picked. The letters "H.O." stand for "hammer-on." (Not all publications use this abbreviation.)

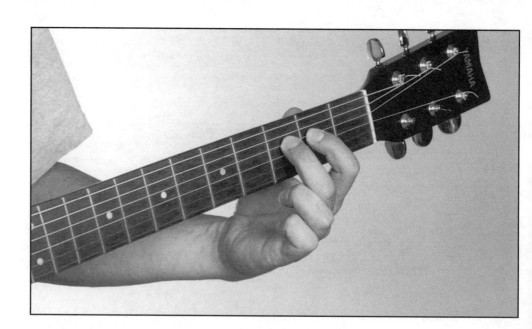

A hammer-on to an *open* string is done like this:

1. Strike an open string such as A with the pick.

2. Bring the 2nd finger down on the A string at the 2nd fret with a fast, hard, hammering motion, and keep it there. The note B will sound without picking the string a second time.

Here it is in music notation:

"John Hardy" and "Old Blue" are written in *cut time* (also called *alla breve*). The symbol for this is ₵, which means that the music is counted two beats to a measure. Every note value is cut by half: whole notes get two beats, half notes get one beat, quarter notes get a half beat, and so on.

John Hardy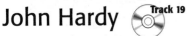

Calypso  Track 21

Calypso is Caribbean music of West African derivation. It was originally a means of social commentary sung over a rhythmic background and is a direct ancestor of today's rap music. A more Americanized type of calypso became popular in the 1950s through the recordings of Harry Belafonte and others. These records featured the guitar in a prominent rhythmic role, but not usually as a solo instrument. Since most calypso songs use only a few chords, students can learn to play calypso music by mastering the rhythm pattern.

To start, play the following strum (follow the picking carefully).

Now, omit the strum played on beat 3.

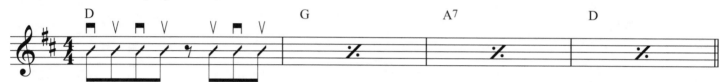

As you can see, the tricky part is leaving out the third beat and playing the two up-picks in a row.

Here are some typical calypso chord progressions. Practice them until you can play them without missing a beat, then try the songs on the next page.

Occasionally, the chord must be changed in the middle of a measure. When this happens, change on the "&" of beat 2, as in the example below.

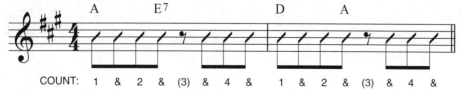

Hey Lolly Lolly

Track 22 Student to learn both the strum and solo parts.

Traditional calypso song

Hey lol - ly, lol-ly lol - ly, hey lol - ly, lol-ly lo,___

hey lol - ly, lol-ly lol - ly, hey lol - ly, lol - ly lo.___ *Fine*

First you sing___ a sim - ple line,___ hey lol - ly, lol-ly lo,___

then you try___ and make it rhyme,___ hey lol - ly, lol - ly lo.___ *D.C. al Fine*

The Sloop "John B."

Track 23

Calypso tempo

Introduction

TEACHER:

Traditional calypso song

So

hoist up the John B. sails,___ see how the main sail set,

send for the cap-tain a - shore let___ me go home.___ Oh, let___ me go

home,___ please let___ me go home, I

feel so break_ up, I wan - na go home.

Key of D Minor

As you have already learned, the key signature of one flat signifies the key of F major. It can also indicate the key of D minor, which is called the *relative minor* key of F major. The one flat in the key signature means that all B's are played as B♭'s unless preceded by a natural sign.

Here are three different D minor scales. Follow the fingering carefully, and add them to your daily practice routine.

D NATURAL MINOR SCALE   Track 24

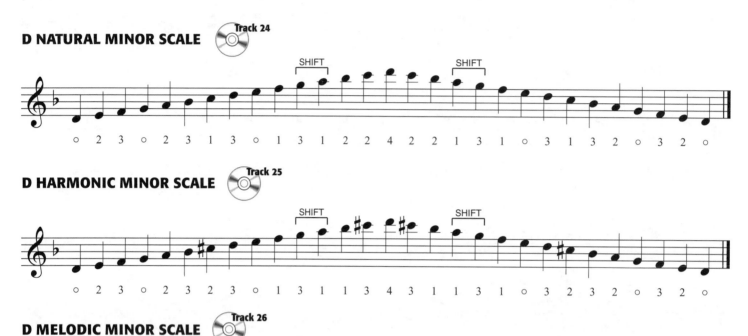

D HARMONIC MINOR SCALE   Track 25

D MELODIC MINOR SCALE   Track 26

Notice that when this scale descends, the sixth and seventh notes of the scale are lowered a half step.

The Three Principal Chords in D Minor with Bass Notes

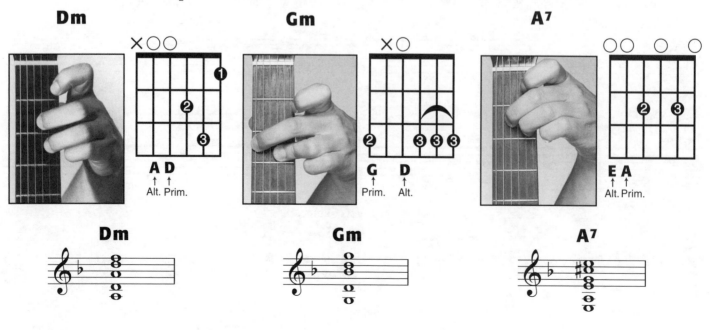

Sicilian Tarantella Track 27

A *tarantella* is a dance of Italian origin that supposedly mimics the movements of someone who has been bitten by a tarantula. This tarantella is very popular and often performed at Italian weddings.

Sixteenth Notes and $\frac{6}{8}$ Time

As in $\frac{2}{4}$, $\frac{3}{4}$ and $\frac{4}{4}$ time, in time, sixteenth notes are played twice as fast as eighth notes.
Compare the following:

The old folk song "The House of the Rising Sun" became a big hit in the 1960s using this accompaniment in $\frac{6}{8}$ time. This accompaniment may be used with the arrangement of "The House of the Rising Sun" on the following page. (Hold chords as much as possible.)

The House of the Rising Sun (duet)

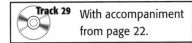 Track 29 With accompaniment from page 22.

Student to learn both parts.

Traditional

Slow and bluesy

HOLD CHORDS WHEREVER POSSIBLE

Key of E Major

The key signature of four sharps indicates the key of E major. Although at first the student may find the number of sharps confusing, it is well worth the effort to master this key, because it is the key in which the guitar sounds best. Many of the best-known blues, country, folk, and rock songs are in the key of E for this reason.

The key signature of four sharps means that all F's are played as F♯'s, all C's are played as C♯'s, all G's are played as G♯'s, and all D's are played as D♯'s. Those are all the sharps in the key of A, plus D♯.

When learning the two-octave E major scale below, follow the fingering carefully. Like all scales, this one should be practiced daily.

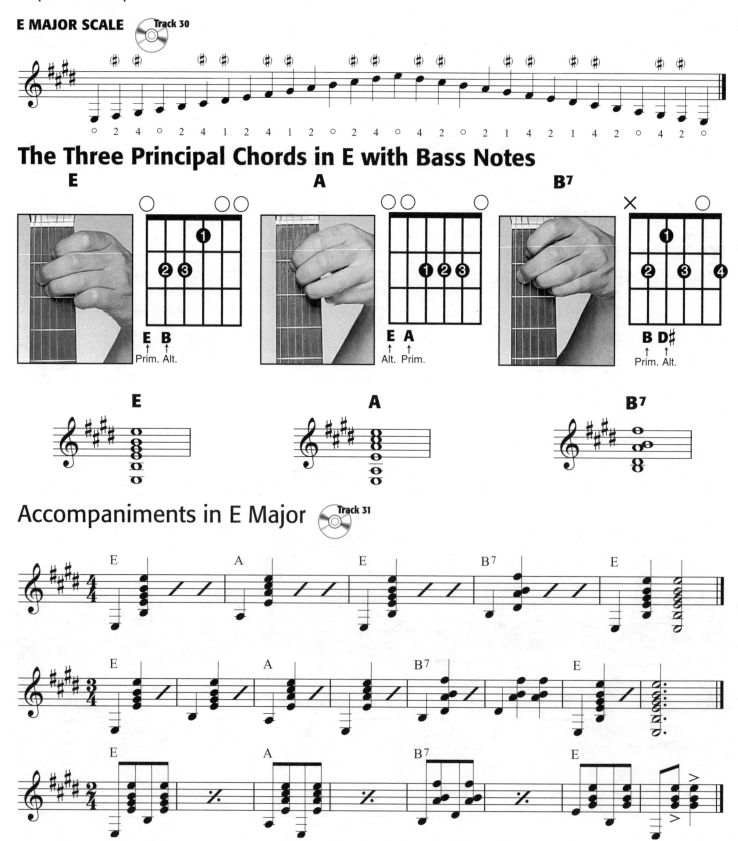

E MAJOR SCALE Track 30

The Three Principal Chords in E with Bass Notes

E   A   B⁷

Accompaniments in E Major Track 31

Finger Exercise in E

Track 32

A valuable exercise for the 2nd and 4th fingers. Remember that F, C, G, and D are sharp.

The Blue Tail Fly

Track 33

The student should learn both the solo part and accompaniment of this famous American folk song.

In the *verse*, each chord should be strummed once where it appears. Tempo is free in this part.

In the *chorus*, also called the *refrain*, play a perky bass/chord accompaniment similar to the one in $\frac{2}{4}$ time on the preceding page.

* This mark (//) is called a *caesura* in classical music. Pop musicians call them "railroad tracks." They mean to leave an extra pause between the two notes.

Using Passing Notes in the Bass

As you have learned, the bass/chord style of accompaniment is generally more effective than just strumming a chord on each beat. The bass notes used are the *root* (the name of the chord), the *5th*, and sometimes the *3rd* of the chord. The chart below shows the various choices of bass note for every chord that you've learned.

Name of Chord	Root	5th	3rd
C	C	G	E
C7	C	G	E
F	F	C	A
G	G	D	B
G7	G	D	B
G minor	G	D	B♭
D	D	A	F#
D7	D	A	F#
D minor	D	A	F
A	A	E	C#
A7	A	E	C#
A minor	A	E	C
E	E	B	G#
E7	E	B	G#
E minor	E	B	G
B7	B	F#	D#

Generally, the root should be your first choice, although when playing 7th chords, it is often more effective to use an alternate note first. Your second choice can be dictated by how easy it is to get to it. For example, the note E in a C chord is the 3rd of that chord, and it is easier to get to than the note G, which is the 5th.

Track 34 Sometimes, it is effective to use *passing notes* to connect the ordinary bass notes of a chord. Passing notes are notes that do not belong to the chord, but connect the notes that do belong to it (the root, 5th or 3rd), usually by step. Here are some examples of various styles.

Diminished 7th Chords

So far, all the chords you have learned belong to three different families: major, minor, and 7th. Another type of chord common in jazz, classical, and pop music is the *diminished 7th* chord. Diminished 7th chords can be derived from ordinary 7th chords by flatting every note in the 7th chord except the root.

D⁷

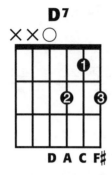

Starting with D7, we have the notes D (root), F# (3rd), A (5th), and C (7th).

D A C F#

Ddim7

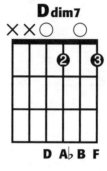

To make a D7 into a D diminished 7th chord, flat the 3rd, 5th, and 7th a half step. This gives us the notes D, F, A♭, and C♭ (or B).

D A♭ B F

A⁷

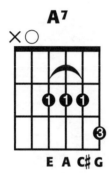

Starting with A7, we have the notes A (root), C# (3rd), E (5th), and G (7th).

E A C# G

Adim7

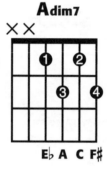

To make an A7 into an A diminished 7th chord, flat the 3rd, 5th, and 7th a half step. This gives us the notes A, C, E♭, and G♭ (or F#).

E♭ A C F#

E⁷

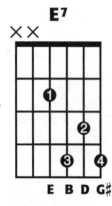

Starting with E7, we have the notes E (root), G# (3rd), B (5th), and D (7th).

E B D G#

Edim7

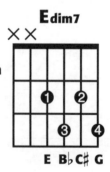

To make an E7 into an E diminished 7th chord, flat the 3rd, 5th, and 7th a half step. This gives us the notes E, G, B♭, and D♭ (or C#).

E B♭ C# G

The good news is that these three diminished chords can be used for every diminished chord in music:

D dim7 = F dim7 = A♭ or G# dim7 = B dim7

A dim7 = C dim7 = E♭ or D# dim7 = G♭ or F# dim7

E dim7 = G dim7 = B♭ dim7 = D♭ or C# dim7

For a bass note, pick any low note in the diminished 7th chord that moves smoothly to your next bass note.

You Tell Me Your Dream (solo with diminished chords)

Moderate Dixieland jazz tempo

Pull-offs  Track 36

The *pull-off* effect is very common in all types of music, but especially in rock, heavy metal, country, blues, and jazz. Like the hammer-on (see page 16), the pull-off allows you to play a note without using the right hand.

A pull-off to a *fingered* string is done like this:

1. Start with a fingered note such as G on the 1st string, 3rd fret.

2. Pick the 1st string with the 1st and 3rd fingers on F and G.

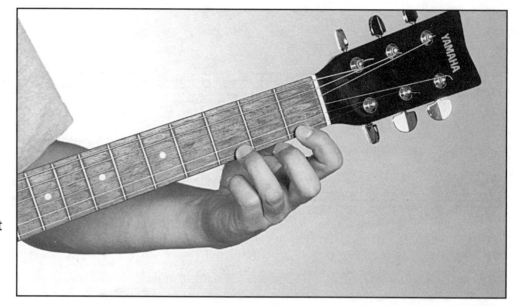

3. Pull the 3rd finger off the string with a lateral motion so that the F sounds clearly.

In music notation, this is written like this:

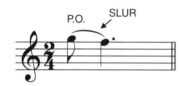

The curved line between the G and the F is a *slur*, which means that the F is not picked. The letters "P.O." stand for "pull-off." (Not all publications use this notation.)

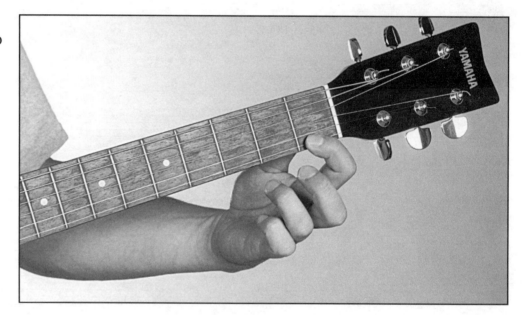

A pull-off to an *open* string is done like this:

1. Start with a fingered note such as G on the 1st string, 3rd fret.

2. Pick the 1st string with the 3rd finger on G.

3. Pull the 3rd finger off the string using a lateral motion so that the open E sounds clearly.

Here it is in music notation:

Country Dance (study with pull-offs)

Track 37

Allegretto

Blues in A (study with pull-offs and hammer-ons)

Track 38

Moderately

The Polka  **Track 39**

As its name implies, the *polka* was originally a Polish dance. It was brought to the United States in the 19th century and still enjoys popularity. The following polka is based on the folk song "Little Brown Jug."

Bright and spirited

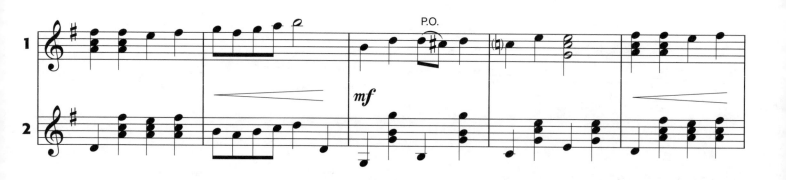

Grace Notes

A *grace note* is a small note (usually an eighth note) with a slash mark through the flag placed before a normal-sized note, like this:

The grace note is played very light and fast (not accented) just before the regular note.

On the guitar, grace notes are played three different ways:

1. From below, as a quick hammer-on using two fingers.

2. From above, as a quick pull-off using two fingers.

3. From either below or above, as a quick slide (see page 38) from the grace note to the regular note using one finger.

Grace notes can be very effective in adding sparkle to a melody, and guitarists like them because they sound good and are easy to play. Although it would be possible to play grace notes before every note in a melody, this would soon become an irritating mannerism, and the tasteful player will limit the use of grace notes to a few effective places.

Amazing Grace Notes   Track 40

In the following study, play the grace notes whichever way is most comfortable and sounds best to you.

Colonel Bogey

Track 41

This great march became popular after its use in the movie classic *The Bridge on the River Kwai*.
Follow the fingering carefully on the grace notes.

March

Kenneth J. Alford

NOTE: E♯ IS THE SAME AS F♮, 1st STRING, 1st FRET

Augmented Chords

To *augment* something means to make it larger. In music, an *augmented* chord is one in which the interval from the root to the 5th has been made larger by a half step.

C

Starting with the C major chord, we have C (root), E (3rd), and G (5th).

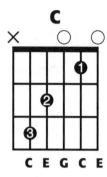

C E G C E

Caug

To make a C major chord into a C augmented chord, raise the 5th a half step, to G#.

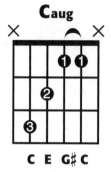

C E G#C

G

Starting with a G major chord, we have G (root), B (3rd), and D (5th).

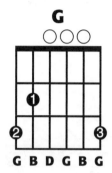

G B D G B G

Gaug

To make a G major chord into a G augmented chord, raise the 5th a half step, to D#.

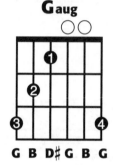

G B D#G B G

F

Starting with an F major chord, we have F (root), A (3rd), and C (5th).

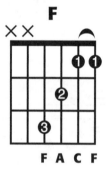

F A C F

Faug

To make an F major chord into an F augmented chord, raise the 5th a half step, to C#.

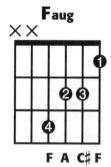

F A C#F

D

Starting with a D major chord, we have D (root), F# (3rd), and A (5th).

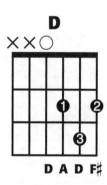

D A D F#

Daug

To make a D major chord into a D augmented chord, raise the 5th a half step, to A#.

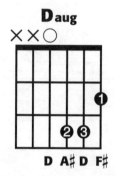

D A#D F#

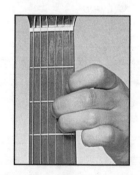

The good news is that these four chords can be used for every augmented chord in music:

C augmented	=	E augmented	=	G# or A♭ augmented
G augmented	=	B augmented	=	D# or E♭ augmented
F augmented	=	A augmented	=	C# or D♭ augmented
D augmented	=	F# augmented	=	A# or B♭ augmented

Track 42 Augmented chords are used most prominently in jazz music. The following chord progressions are typical of the way augmented chords are used.

IMPORTANT: In modern sheet music, augmented chords are usually indicated by a plus sign (for example C+, G+ and so on).

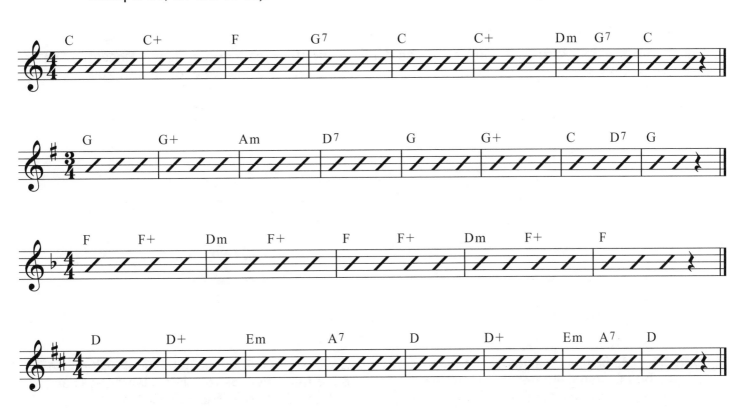

The following chord progression fits the melody of the great Duke Ellington standard "Take the A Train." Note the extensive use of augmented chords.

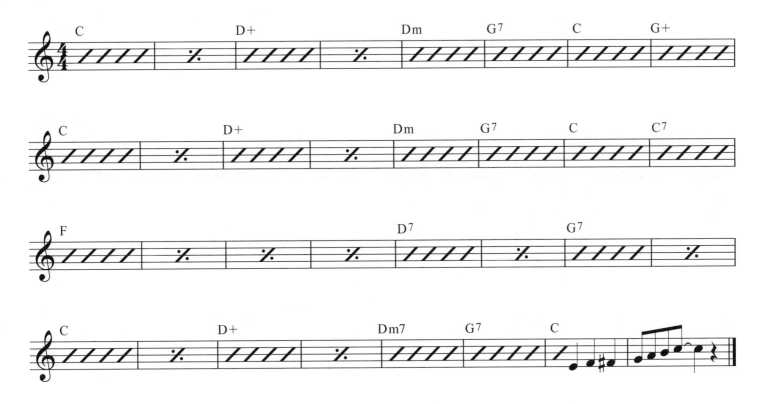

Slides  Track 43

Sliding up to or away from a note is a very common and effective device.

1. Sliding from one note to another must always be done on one string, either up or down. Finger the first note and pick the string. Then, without releasing the pressure on the string, slide to the next note.

In musical notation:

2. Often, the slide begins on an indefinite note a few frets above or below the final note. Start with a little pressure on the string, but not enough to press it down to the fret. Then, as you slide toward the final note, gradually increase the pressure so that when you reach the final note, it sounds clear.

3. Sliding away from a definite note to an indefinite note is more or less the reverse of no. 2 above. Start with any note that is at least five frets up the fingerboard. Pick the string, and as you slide down and away from the note, gradually release the pressure on the string so that your finger stops its vibration.

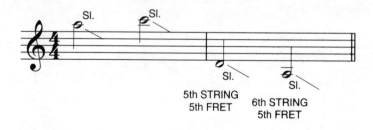

Slidin' Around (duet) Track 44

This duet demonstrates the use of slides in blues playing. For best results, the student should learn both parts. If playing alone, play the 2nd part first, then the 1st part, then the 2nd part again to finish up. If playing as a duet, have the 2nd player play the arrangement through once, then add the top part. More advanced players will want to improvise some blues against the funky bass line.

Moderate funky blues

Tunes That Teach Technic No. 2

Devil's Dream Hornpipe 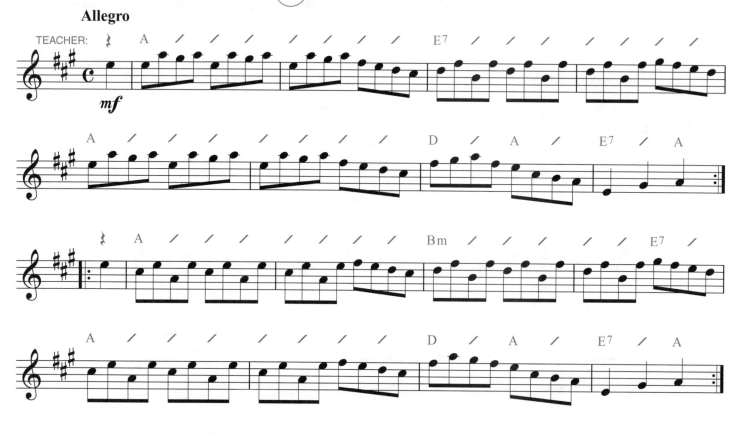 Track 45

Our Katie (oberek) 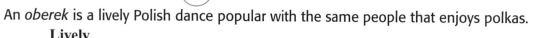 Track 46

An *oberek* is a lively Polish dance popular with the same people that enjoys polkas.

Abide with Me (duet) Track 47

This arrangement of the lovely old hymn combines a chord/melody solo in the 1st part with an arpeggio-style accompaniment in the 2nd part. The student should learn both parts. Also, note that the accompaniment is always played at a dynamic one level lower than the melody part.

The tempo indication *Lento* means to play slowly.

Words by
Henry Francis Lyte

Music by
William H. Monk

HOLD FINGERS DOWN AS LONG AS POSSIBLE

Beguine

The *beguine* (be-GEEN) is a graceful dance of Afro-Cuban origin that became known in the U.S. around 1930 and has remained popular ever since. Its rhythm makes ingenious use of the bass/chord style on guitar, breaking up the bass notes and the chords in a syncopated pattern that gives the dance its characteristic sound.

Here is the basic rhythm of the beguine:

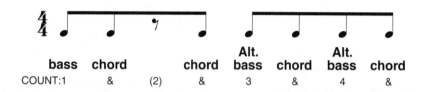

Notice that the pattern is simply a bass/chord pattern played in eighth notes, but with the second bass note omitted. It is this omission of the second downbeat that gives the rhythm of the beguine its characteristic sound.

First, practice the beguine rhythm on the D and A7 chords as written out below. Then, learn both the melody (part 1) and the accompaniment (part 2) of the beautiful Italian beguine "Guitarra Romana."

Track 48

Guitarra Romana (Roman Guitar) Track 49

Eldo di Lazzaro

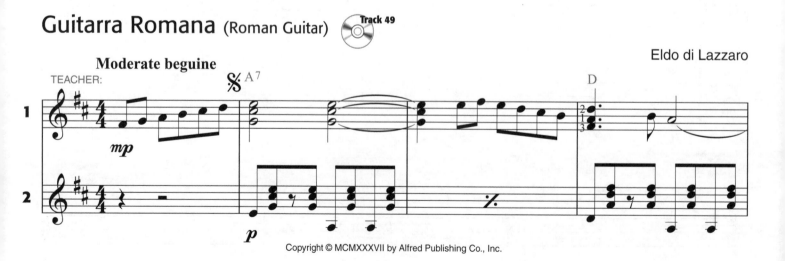

For a very nice effect during the following interlude, guitar 1 can lightly muffle the strings with the heel of the right hand. This produces a sound like that of pizzicato strings.

Bends

The laws of acoustics state that when the tension of a string is increased, its pitch rises. Blues players discovered this in the early days of blues, and the technic, now called *bending* a string, has become standard. Here's how to do it.

1. Finger any note on any of the first five strings and pick the string; for example, use the note E on the 2nd string, 5th fret.

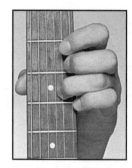

2. Keeping the pressure on the string, push it across the fingerboard until you hear the pitch rise a half step, from E to F.

Bends do not work well on the lower frets, so make sure the note you're bending is at least on the 3rd fret or higher. Also, make sure you're using a light-gauge string. It's difficult to do this effect if the string is too stiff.

Modern heavy metal players often bend notes a whole step, 1 ½ steps, and even 2 steps higher. This can be accomplished by using an extremely light-gauge string, such as .008s, and playing up around the 12th fret.

When bending notes on the low E, the string must be pulled to avoid pushing it off the fingerboard.

Play A on the 6th string, 5th fret.

Bend A to A♯.

Unfortunately for the student, the notation of this effect is still in contention. Some arrangers write the fingered note and indicate by using an arrow that it should be bent up a ½ step or more. Others prefer to write the final pitch with a notation to bend it up from a lower note. In this book we use the former notation.

Bending the Blues Track 50

Pistol Pete Track 51

The arrow with 1/4 above it is often used to tell the performer to pull the note up a quarter of a step, that is, not quite up to the next note. One advantage that guitar players have over piano players is that they can play these sounds, which do not exist on a piano.

Counterpoint

The word *counterpoint* means two or more melodies are played at the same time. Of course, the idea is that they sound good together. In classical music, the unquestioned master of counterpoint was the great J. S. Bach (1685–1750), who thought nothing of improvising four- and five-part fugues. Counterpoint hasn't been used much in popular music, but occasionally a little gem turns up, like "Simple Melody" by Irving Berlin. In this one, he manages to write two different melodies that sound good individually or when played simultaneously.

The following arrangement can be played in several ways. Either of the parts marked 1 and 2 can be played as a solo or as a solo accompanied by part 3; or, all three parts can be played simultaneously.

Simple Melody (trio) Track 52

Irving Berlin

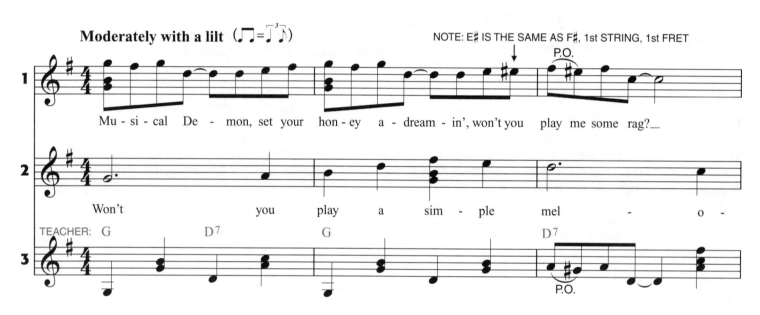

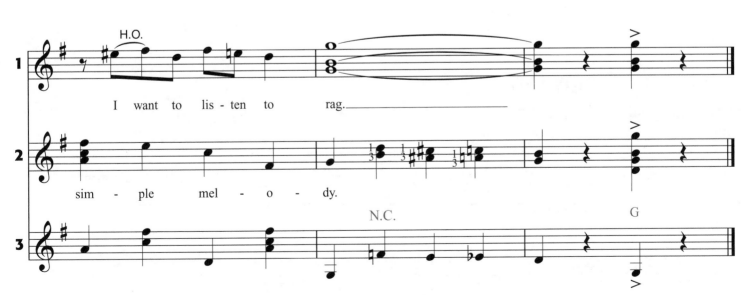

Tunes That Teach Technic No. 3

Here we will combine pull-offs and hammer-ons in ways common to rock, blues, and jazz guitarists. Concentrate on articulating clearly, that is, make sure each note sounds clear regardless of whether or not it is picked.

Onyx Club Hop   Track 53

Just Lopin' Along   Track 54

Jingle for a Sunny Day   Track 55